Teeth

WAYLAND

First published in 2008
by Wayland

Copyright © Wayland 2008

Wayland
338 Euston Road
London NW1 3BH

Wayland Australia
Level 17/207 Kent Street
Sydney NSW 2000

Senior Editor: Jennifer Schofield
Designer: Sophie Pelham
Digital Colour: Carl Gordon

CIP data:
 Gogerly, Liz
   Teeth. - (Looking after me)
   1. Teeth - Care and hygiene - Juvenile literature
   I. Title
   617.6'01

ISBN: 978 0 7502 5304 8
Printed in China

Wayland is a division of Hachette Children's Books,
an Hachette Livre UK company.

Looking After Me

Teeth

Written by Liz Gogerly
Illustrated by Mike Gordon

WAYLAND

I love my dog Billy. Whenever he was good, I gave him doggy chocolate drops and biscuits.

One day when Billy was yawning,
I saw something black in his mouth.

We took Billy to the vet. He needed to have the bad tooth taken out!

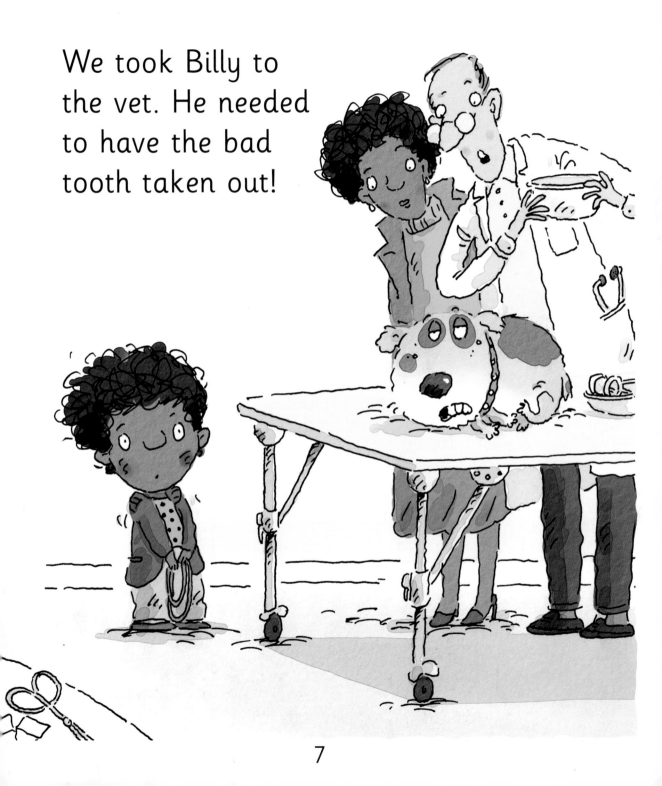

The vet said that he shouldn't eat any more chocolate and he gave us a dog toothbrush and toothpaste.

Billy hated having his teeth
cleaned, but we didn't want
him to loose any more of them.

He needed his
teeth to eat,

to chew dad's
slippers,

and to keep his tongue in place!

Instead of chocolates, we gave
Billy juicy bones.

Soon he had sparkly white teeth
and healthy pink gums.

But I didn't.

My front tooth was wobbling.
Very soon, it was going to fall out.

I didn't want a gap like Billy's.

Nor did I want all my teeth to rot.

And, I definitely didn't want any of Billy's chicken-flavoured toothpaste.

Mum told me not to worry.

She said that
as we grow
older our baby
teeth fall out.

Our new adult teeth must last for ever, so it's important that we look after them .

You should brush your teeth with fluoride toothpaste every morning and night.

Food and drinks leave a sticky layer of white stuff on your teeth, called plaque.

18

Plaque and sugar make
your teeth decay.

When you brush
your teeth, you get
rid of the plaque
and sugar.

This helps
keep your
teeth and
gums
healthy.

I've discovered that teeth are amazing things. They are covered with a hard layer called enamel.

enamel

dentine

gum

nerves

You also have different kinds of teeth.

You have canines for tearing, incisors for cutting and molars for chewing.

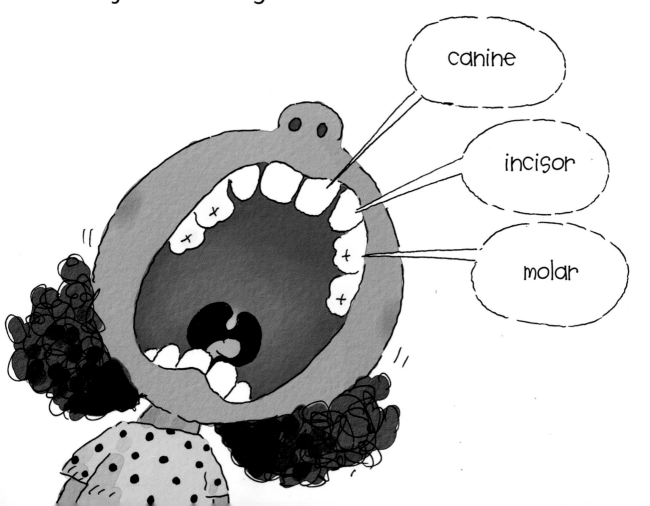

You must look after your teeth.
It all begins with brushing.

Mum buys me a
new toothbrush
every three months.

And, I never ever share
my brush with anyone!

Now I visit the dentist regularly.
She checks my teeth for decay.

If you have a bad tooth then your dentist may need to give you a filling.

Eating healthy food is also important for looking after your teeth.

At snack time I eat fruit,

vegetables or cheese.

I drink water, especially between meals.

And, if I have a sugary drink, then I use a straw.

Now, when a tooth falls out,
I don't worry any more.

I pop it under my pillow and wait for the tooth fairy to leave me a shiny new coin!

NOTES FOR PARENTS AND TEACHERS

SUGGESTIONS FOR READING **LOOKING AFTER ME: TEETH** WITH CHILDREN

In this story we meet a young girl, Marta, who learns that part of living a healthy lifestyle is learning about our teeth and how we look after them properly. Not looking after our teeth can lead to rotten teeth or fillings. In this story it is Marta's dog, Billy, who suffers from a bad tooth. The idea of a dog needing dental treatment and having its teeth cleaned may be quite amusing for children. It is also a good way to initiate discussion about what the children think causes dental decay. Billy has been eating too many chocolates. The children will probably pick up on this and they may also have their own ideas about why Billy has a bad tooth.

Once Billy's tooth is removed, the vet instructs Marta to brush his teeth. This is a good opportunity to discuss the importance of cleaning our teeth twice a day. The British Dental Health Foundation (BDHF) gives advice about how to brush children's teeth, as well as other useful information about looking after teeth at: www.dentalhealth.org.uk. The BDHF also suggests that children need assistance in cleaning their teeth until they are at least seven years old. You could point out that Billy has to be helped to clean his teeth.

Losing our first teeth, or baby teeth, is part of childhood. Unfortunately, Marta is confused and thinks that a wobbly tooth is a rotten tooth. The book aims to reassure children that losing their first teeth is normal and that these first teeth are replaced by adult teeth, which must last a lifetime. This is a good point to start talking about visiting the dentist for regular check-ups.

The text is filled with ways in which we can care for our teeth and perhaps the children have some ideas of their own. Together with the children you could come up with a list of new resolutions to look after their own teeth.

LOOKING AFTER ME AND THE NATIONAL CURRICULUM

The Looking After Me series of books is aimed at children studying PSHE at Key Stage 1. In the section *Knowledge, Skills and Understanding: Developing a Healthy, Safer Lifestyle* of the National Curriculum, it is stated that pupils are expected to 'learn about themselves as developing individuals and as members of their communities, building on their own experiences and on the early learning goals for personal, social and emotional development'.

Children are expected to learn:
- how to make simple choices that improve their health and well-being to maintain personal hygiene;
- how some diseases spread and can be controlled;
- about the process of growing from young to old and how people's needs change;
- the names of the main parts of the body;
- that all household products, including medicines, can be harmful if not used properly;
- rules for, and ways of, keeping safe, including basic road safety, and about people who can help them to stay safe.

31

BOOKS TO READ

I Know Why I Brush My Teeth Kate Rowan (Walker Books, 2000)
Why Must I Brush My Teeth? Jackie Gaff (Cherrytree Books, 2004)
My Wobbly Tooth Must Not Ever Never Fall Out Lauren Child
(Puffin Books, 2006)

ACTIVITY

This activity can be done as a whole-class project or individually. Children look for pictures of different animals in which they can see the animals' teeth. They then need to guess what kind of food the animals eat by looking at the teeth. For example, lions are carnivores and their teeth are sharp and suited to eating meat, while cows are herbivores and so have large, flat teeth, suitable for eating grass.

INDEX